HAUNTED OR HOAX?

HAUNTED WOODS AND CAVES

JANICE DYER

CRABTREE
PUBLISHING COMPANY
WWW.CRABTREEBOOKS.COM

HAUNTED OR HOAX?

Author: Janice Dyer

Editors: Marcia Abramson, Petrice Custance

Photo research: Melissa McClellan

Cover/interior design: T.J. Choleva

Proofreader: Lorna Notsch

Production coordinator and
prepress technician: Tammy McGarr

Print coordinator: Katherine Berti

Consultant: Susan Demeter-St. Clair
Paranormal Studies & Inquiry

Written and produced for Crabtree Publishing by
BlueAppleWorks Inc.

Photographs & Illustrations

Cover illustration: T.J Choleva (background image: Merydolla/Shutterstock; left image Annette Shaff/
Shutterstock);Title page illustration: Joshua Avramson (background image: Nikki Zalewski/Shutterstock;
left imagemaradon 333/Shutterstock)
Shutterstock.com: © Login (page backgrounds); © Denis Belitsky (p. 4 top right); © Fer Gregory (p. 4
bottom right, 6 bottom left); © Venus © Kaewyoo (p. 5 middle); © andreiuc88 (p. 5, 9, 13, 15 sidebar); ©
szarkazsofi (p.6–7 bottom); © Buffy1982 (p. 7 top); © Edvard Mizsei (p. 7 bottom right); © Ensuper (p. 9,
19); © H1nksy (p. 10 right); © dugdax (p. 11, 23 sidebar); © Daniel Mirlea (p. 12 top right); © maradon
333 (p. 12 left); © Nikki Zalewski (p. 12–13 bottom); © eddtoro/Shutterstock.com (p. 13 bottom right); ©
Mikadun (p. 14 bottom right);
© Lev Kropotov (p. 15 middle); © andreiuc88 (p. 15 sidebar); © Berke (p. 16 bottom left);
© vladimir salman (p. 15 bottom middle); © e2dan (p. 17 left); © Steve Oehlenschlager
(p. 18 bottom left); © Triff (p. 19 sidebar); © happystock (p. 20 top right); © Maximum Exposure PR (p. 20
bottom left); © Scott Biales (p. 20 bottom); © Evgenyrychko (p. 21 bottom middle); © Aleksey Stemmer (p.
21 sidebar); © Zack Frank (p. 24 top right); © Andrey_Kuzmin (p. 25 middle); © Basileus (p. 25, 27 sidebar);
© MilanMarkovic78 (p. 26 right);
© Dina Julayeva (p. 28); © alsamua (p. 29 middle right)
Creative Commons: John S Turner (p. 10 bottom right); Tare Gheorghe (p. 14 top right inset); Markus 'Mex'
Winkler (p. 18 top right); Daniel Schwen (p. 22 bottom); Dave Bunnell (p. 24 right); Stuart Logan (p. 25
bottom right); Itto Ogami (p. 27 right)
Public Domain: Ivan Kramskoi (p. 5 bottom right); Davis (p. 9 top left); p. 9 bottom left; Patrons'
Permanent Fund and Chester Dale Fund (p. 11 bottom); Alessandro Magnasco
(p. 19 bottom); NPS Photo (p. 22 left, p. 23 bottom); p. 23 top left
Joshua Avramson p. 6 top right, p. 6–7 bottom, p. 8–9 bottom, p. 14 top right, p. 14 bottom,
p. 18 bottom, p. 21 bottom, p. 24, p. 29
Carlyn Iverson p. 8 right, p. 11 right (background image: Claude-Joseph Vernet/Public Domain); p. 16
bottom right, p. 26–27, p. 29 right

Library and Archives Canada Cataloguing in Publication

Dyer, Janice, author
       Haunted woods and caves / Janice Dyer.

(Haunted or hoax?)
Includes index.
Issued in print and electronic formats.
ISBN 978-0-7787-4637-9 (hardcover).--
ISBN 978-0-7787-4643-0 (softcover).--
ISBN 978-1-4271-2056-4 (HTML)

       1. Haunted places--Juvenile literature. 2. Forests and forestry--
Juvenile literature. 3. Caves--Juvenile literature. 4. Ghosts--Juvenile
literature. I. Title.

BF1461.D949 2018   j133.1'22   C2017-907790-2
                                                          C2017-907791-0

Library of Congress Cataloging-in-Publication Data

Names: Dyer, Janice, author.
Title: Haunted woods and caves / Janice Dyer.
Description: New York : Crabtree Publishing Company, 2018. |
  Series: Haunted or hoax? | Includes index.
Identifiers: LCCN 2018000097 (print) | LCCN 2018000754 (ebook) |
  ISBN 9781427120564 (Electronic) |
  ISBN 9780778746379 (hardcover : alk. paper) |
  ISBN 9780778746430 (pbk. : alk. paper)
Subjects: LCSH: Haunted places--Juvenile literature. |
  Ghosts--Juvenile literature.
Classification: LCC BF1461 (ebook) | LCC BF1461 .D94 2018 (print) |
  DDC 133.1/22--dc23
LC record available at https://lccn.loc.gov/2018000097

Crabtree Publishing Company

www.crabtreebooks.com   1-800-387-7650

Printed in the U.S.A./032018/BG20180202

Published in Canada
Crabtree Publishing
616 Welland Ave.
St. Catharines, Ontario
L2M 5V6

Published in the United States
Crabtree Publishing
PMB 59051
350 Fifth Avenue, 59th Floor
New York, New York 10118

Published in the United Kingdom
Crabtree Publishing
Maritime House
Basin Road North, Hove
BN41 1WR

Published in Australia
Crabtree Publishing
3 Charles Street
Coburg North
VIC, 3058

CONTENTS

FEARSOME FOREST GHOSTS

Imagine walking through a deep, dark forest at night. You hear rustling in the leaves and other strange and spooky sounds. You see a glowing shape moving in the distance. Is it the wind? An animal? Or could it be a ghost?

Fear of the Unknown

Throughout history, people have told stories of ghosts and ghostly sightings in forests and caves. They made up the stories and **myths** to explain things they didn't understand. These stories were then passed down through the ages.

Fairy tales often take place in dark forests of twisted trees. *Folklore* experts think these tales got started, in part, to warn people of real dangers in the woods.

Some forests and caves are said to be haunted because of battles or crimes that happened there in the past. Others may be ancient burial grounds, where the spirits of the dead continue to linger. No matter the reason, many think that forests and caves around the world are haunted.

Tales of the Paranormal

Paranormal forces may explain some of the ghost sightings in forests and caves. A paranormal event cannot be explained by normal experiences or science. Things like ghosts, unidentified flying objects (UFOs), **psychic** abilities, and **extraterrestrials** are all called paranormal.

Is there any **evidence** that ghosts really exist? Paranormal investigators collect samples, or data, so they can try to find an explanation for an event. To prove that a ghost exists, they may use technology, such as cameras, sound recorders, motion detectors, or video recordings. However, most of the evidence for ghosts is based on **anecdotal** evidence, or people's stories, rather than on scientific proof.

Even though there is little scientific evidence and some of the stories are hoaxes, people continue to tell ghost stories as though they were true.

RUSALKI – THE MARSH NYMPHS

Rusalki, or water **nymphs**, are spirits that are often seen around lakes, rivers, ponds, **marshes**, swamps, and other bodies of water. They have pale skin and long hair and wear long flowing robes. According to folklore, rusalki are the ghosts of women who died near water when they were young. Their spirits then come back to haunt the waterway. Rusalki spend their time convincing men to come near the water so they can drag them into the water and drown them. They lure their victims into marshes by lighting lanterns and calling out to follow them in. Some countries honor the rusalki during a week in June when the rusalki are said to come on shore to play in the trees and dance in the moonlight. People make sure not to go swimming during this time, for fear the rusalki will drag them underwater to their death.

Rusalki have legs rather than a mermaid's fish tail. They can dance and climb trees.

THE CURSED FOREST OF MASSACHUSETTS

Weird things happen in the Freetown State Forest near Boston. The forest is located in the middle of the Bridgewater Triangle. Locals have seen unidentified flying objects (UFOs), **Bigfoot**, ghosts, and mysterious lights in the area. Others report strange disappearances. The Freetown State Forest is also known as the Cursed Forest of Massachusetts.

The Bridgewater Triangle is located about 30 miles (48 km) south of Boston. The name was likely inspired by the famously spooky **Bermuda Triangle**.

On May 10, 1760, witnesses reported seeing a "sphere of fire" in the area that was brighter than the Sun. In 1968, people saw a large ball of light floating in the trees.

Killing Grounds

Murders, crimes, and weird rituals have taken place in the area over the years. Several murders happened in the forest, including one young local girl who was kidnapped and killed there. People also have found mysterious clearings in the forest stained with animal blood, along with the bodies of dead cattle. Perhaps these are signs of animal sacrifices?

Some people say Freetown State Forest will stay cursed until all the land is returned to the Native peoples who used to live there.

Dark Power

The Bridgewater Triangle covers 200 square miles (520 square km). It has been a magnet for paranormal activity since the 1700s. Along with ghosts, UFOs, and Bigfoot, a giant snake is said to appear every seven years. Many believe that the forest gives off a dark power that drives people to suicide.

DID YOU KNOW?

From the 1600s, the forest was the site of conflict between European settlers and the Native peoples who lived there. It's said that the forest became cursed as the land was taken unfairly from Native peoples. In 1939, the state gave back less than 1 square mile (3 square km) of land.

Paranormal Events

So many strange events have happened in the forest that it's hard to list them all. Here are a few of the spookiest:

Native peoples in the area say the forest is home to troll-like creatures called Pukwudgies. They say these creatures like to startle people by throwing sand in their faces, but sometimes they can be violent—pushing people over cliffs or attacking them with knives.

Hockomock Swamp is said to be another haunted area of the forest. The name means "place where the spirits dwell." Reports of ghosts, UFOs, and strange hairy creatures in the swamp are common. Others say they have seen a huge birdlike creature.

Bigfoot often stomps through the Hockomock Swamp, according to some reports from witnesses. Most say the creature, also known as Sasquatch, is peaceful. In the 1970s, though, local farmers thought a hairy monster was killing their animals. Police searched with tracking dogs but found nothing—not even a hungry bear.

Eerie Rocks and Cliffs

Visitors report seeing ghosts jumping from the Assonet Ledge, which drops 80 feet (24 m) into a rock **quarry**.

Others report seeing glowing balls of light and hearing voices at Profile Rock. This 50-foot (15-m) rock in the forest is shaped like a human face. Some people claim to have seen a ghostly figure of a man sitting on the rock. Others have seen "ghost dancers" performing ceremonial dances there.

Dighton Rock, a huge boulder in the forest, is covered in mysterious drawings and writing. Nobody knows who made the drawings or what they mean.

HAUNTED NIAGARA: SCREAMING TUNNEL

The Screaming Tunnel was built in the early 1800s as a drainage tunnel to remove water from farmland. It runs underneath railway lines near Niagara Falls, Ontario. Local legend says that the tunnel is haunted by the ghost of a young girl who ran screaming into the tunnel to escape a fire or someone who was chasing her. Some say that if you walk to the middle of the tunnel at night and light a wooden match, you will hear the spirit of the girl screaming. The creepy tunnel is now a tourist attraction. It was even used as one of the locations for the filming of a horror movie called *The Dead Zone*.

Dighton Rock in 1893. A museum was built on the shore to house it.

Some people think Profile Rock looks like Massasoit, the famed chief of the Wampanoag nation.

LOOK AT THE EVIDENCE

Evidence of ghost sightings at the Freetown State Forest is based on the anecdotal statements of witnesses. Some investigators have also used cameras, night vision equipment, and other technology to try to record paranormal events. Are you convinced by these stories, or could they be made up to attract tourists to the area?

FOREST THAT DEFIES THE LAWS OF SCIENCE

Epping Forest in Essex, England, has a long history of hauntings. It is believed that the forest has been a protected area since the 1100s. In the 1800s, Queen Victoria declared the area protected "for all time." As a result, Epping Forest is often called "the People's Forest."

Forest Murders

However, the ancient forest has a dark side. Because it is located close to London, it was a popular hideout for criminals over the ages. Many murders have taken place there. More than a dozen victims have been found in the dark woods in the last 50 years alone. Several had been buried. Others were found on the forest floor under that ancient trees.

DID YOU KNOW?

Dick Turpin, a famous **highwayman**, used Epping Forest as a hideout in the 1700s. Turpin was a horse thief, burglar, and killer. A cave in the forest is called Turpin's Cave. Some believe that his ghost continues to haunt the forest.

A church in the Epping Forest District also has a long history of ghostly sightings. Greensted Church (at right) is about 1,200 years old and is the oldest wooden church in the world.

Hangman's Hill and Suicide Pool

Two particular areas in the forest have been the site of most of the paranormal activity: Hangman's Hill and Suicide Pool.

It is said that cars parked at the bottom of Hangman's Hill will slowly roll uphill. Local legend says the cars are being pulled toward an ancient tree where three witches were hanged. Others say an innocent man was hanged there.

Some say an evil force lives at Suicide Pool. According to folklore, a father killed his daughter at the pool 300 years ago because she was meeting a boy there. It is said the boy killed himself at the same spot. No birds are heard near the site, and no animals are seen.

Visitors to Epping Forest report seeing everything from headless horsemen to the ghost of a woman who causes accidents by leaping out in front of cars. Others say they feel like they are being pushed by unseen hands.

PEMBREY WOODS, ENGLAND

Locals say the ancient Pembrey Woods are haunted by victims of "little people with hatchets." This gang of robbers lit lanterns to lure ships to crash on the rocky shore. They looted wrecks and killed survivors with their hatchets. Visitors often report seeing the ghosts of these ships and sailors.

It's still unclear whether the hatchet people of Pembrey were real or a legend.

TRANSYLVANIA'S GATE
TO THE SPIRIT WORLD

The Hoia-Baciu Forest is known as the Bermuda Triangle of Transylvania, Romania. The forest is small—only about 1 square mile (3 square km)—and is located on high ground near a group of small towns. Even though it is small, it is known as the world's most haunted forest. Intense paranormal activity and unexplained events include ghost sightings, strange lights, UFO sightings, and mysterious faces that appear in photographs of the area.

Scientists can't explain why the trees grow in zig-zag patterns or in spirals in the forest.

Fearful Locals

Most locals who live in the area are too scared to enter the forest. They call it an evil place, and believe if they enter the forest they will never return home. Some of those who have been brave enough to enter the forest have reported developing rashes, burns, and scratches.

Eyewitnesses report seeing the souls of peasants roaming the forest surrounded by fog. The forest is also said to have a famous ghost: Vlad Dracula, the cruel ruler who inspired the Dracula legend.

12

Uneasy Feelings

Visitors often say they feel anxious and nauseous while in the forest. Others say they feel like they are being watched. Maybe the strangely shaped trees or unexplained burns on branches are the reason for their anxious feelings.

Visitors say they have seen visions of tormented spirits in the forest. Some say the woods are haunted by Romanian peasants who were murdered there, and the souls of these ghosts are trapped in the forest.

MYSTERIOUS LIGHTS

Flickering balls of light are called ghost orbs or spirit orbs. Some people think they are friendly spirits trying to communicate by dancing and winking on and off. It's said that cats are especially good at seeing ghost orbs!

Paranormal investigators have studied ghost orbs with high-tech equipment. Some are linked to natural causes ranging from static electricity to rocket launches. But many remain a mystery.

Other orbs appear on photos. They may be caused by dust or moisture on the camera lens. Like ghost orbs, though, some are mysteries. One popular idea is that they are guardian angels or spirit guides who take the form of orbs to watch over people.

*Paranormal investigators say electronic devices often stop working in areas that have **supernatural** activity.*

13

Gateway to Spirit World

Some people claim that the forest is a portal, or gateway, to the spirit world. Stories tell of people disappearing in the forest, strange lights appearing above the forest, and wind that seems to speak.

Lost in Time

Some say they experienced missing time when they entered the forest. They became lost in the forest for a period of time but have no memory of how they spent that time. Folklore tells of a five-year-old girl who entered the forest one day and got lost. Her family searched all over but could not find her. Five years later, she turned up in the forest. She was still wearing the clothes she disappeared in. They were not torn or dirty after all that time. Even stranger, she was still five years old. She did not know what had happened and could remember nothing from the lost years. The story is widespread, but no one knows if or when it happened. If there were any records, they too have disappeared.

Given the small size of the forest, do you think a girl could have remained missing for five years?

The haunted forest is named after a shepherd who went missing in the forest with 200 sheep.

14

Haunted Woods

Other stories claim there is a round dead zone in the forest where no vegetation grows. It is said there is no explanation for why plants refuse to grow there. Locals claim this is the center of the paranormal activity in the area.

Some of the stories about the Hoia–Baciu Forest may be exaggerated. However, the sheer amount of unexplained paranormal activity in the area makes experts wonder what could be going on there.

LOOK AT THE EVIDENCE

People have taken photographs of UFOs seen near the Hoia-Baciu Forest. Other photos taken in the area show unexplained faces and images. Paranormal investigators have used a thermal detector. They say that the balls of light seen over the forest do not give off any heat. Since most types of light give off heat, they have no explanation for their findings. Researchers from countries around the world have spent time in the forest studying its mysteries. The forest has also been included on lists for tourists of the most haunted places in the world. Are you convinced by these stories, or could they be made up to attract tourists to the area?

THE UFO HOTBED

The forest may be the gateway to more than just the spirit world. Many people report seeing UFOs in the area. Perhaps it is a portal for aliens, too!

A famous photo was taken in 1968 by biologist Alexandru Swift. It appeared to show a UFO. Similar photos were taken by many others at the same time and into the 1970s.

Another researcher says that medieval drawings and records show an alien spaceship that landed at Dracula's castle. So some people blame aliens for people losing time or going missing in the forest.

A recent view from Google Earth seemed to show a spaceship parked in Romania. But that turned out to be a water tower. So far, no one has proven an alien presence.

WEREWOLVES— THE FOREST DEMONS

The Werewolf of Gévaudan

Between 1764 and 1767, in the Gévaudan region of southern France, about 100 children and women were killed by something locals called "the Beast." Many others were attacked but survived. Witnesses described the beast as having a huge head with razor sharp teeth, and a red coat with black markings. Some said it was as big as a cow!

What Was It?

People living in the area were terrified. They told many stories about the Beast. Some said it was a wolf or a wolf-dog **hybrid**. Others said it was a **werewolf**, a bloodthirsty wolf-like monster. Still others blamed a pack of wolves for the killings.

King of France Sends Help

The residents lived in terror while the Beast attacked people who dared to work alone in the area. In one famous story, Jacques Portfaix and his friends were viciously attacked by the Beast. They stayed together as a group and were able to fight off the animal. The king of France rewarded them for their bravery. He also sent a series of professional wolf hunters to the area to try to kill the creature. The hunters killed a number of large wolves, but the attacks continued.

Mystery Continues

Although we still don't know for sure what this mysterious creature really was, we do know that it killed up to 100 people over four years. People panicked at the time of the attacks. When no cause was found, they turned to supernatural explanations, which soon spread. Experts today suspect that more than one animal was responsible for the killings, possibly a young male lion.

The attacks were brutal. The Beast seemed to deliberately attack people's heads and necks. Could it have been hunting for pleasure rather than food?

Moosham Castle Werewolves

Moosham Castle is one of the most haunted spots in Austria. The castle is famous for its dark history. Thousands of people were accused of being witches and were tortured and executed there. However, Moosham Castle isn't just known for witches—it is also said that supernatural creatures roam its halls.

The stories of werewolves in Moosham Castle started in the 1800s. Similar to the Beast of Gévaudan, a series of animal attacks were reported near the castle. Stories say that a wolf-like creature was killing and **mutilating** deer and cattle.

Moosham Castle was built in the 1100s. It became known as the Witches Castle during the 1700s.

DID YOU KNOW?

Wolf-charmers were people who were believed to use magic to change wolves into werewolves. Like witches, many wolf-charmers were put on trial and often executed.

Confessions Under Torture

Armed hunters were sent out to kill the wolves, but they failed. Some accused locals of being werewolves. Others accused staff members who lived in the castle. The "werewolves" were held captive in the castle and tortured in the dungeons until they confessed. Many said Satan had given them a "black cream" that allowed them to change into wolves. After they confessed, they were executed.

Did the violent and bloody history of the castle attract werewolves to the area? Or did the ghosts in the castle have a terrible effect on those living there? In either case, people say Moosham Castle is haunted even today.

CRUEL AND UNUSUAL PUNISHMENT

Since ancient times, extreme physical pain has been used to get people to make confessions or tell secrets. Torture was even considered a just punishment for some crimes. It is said that the spirits of tortured souls haunt some dungeons and prisons to this day.

"Cruel and unusual punishment," including torture, was banned by England in 1689. The same ban is in the U.S. Bill of Rights. The United Nations adopted a ban on torture in 1948.

The legend of ghosts rattling chains may come from medieval dungeons, where people were chained up for many days.

LOOK AT THE EVIDENCE

Werewolf sightings were most common in the 1500s and 1600s in Europe. Many people were accused of being werewolves, tortured, and executed. The fear that people felt at the time was real, and there is evidence that people and animals were mutilated and killed. But who or what did the killing? Today, most experts are convinced that werewolves are made up. Instead, they blame packs of wolves or other animals for the attacks. What do you think?

THE HEADLESS BOY OF DOW HILL FOREST

The Forest of Dow Hill in Kurseong is one of the most haunted places in India. Headless ghosts, strange sounds, and spooky red eyes—all this and more is said to be found in this creepy area.

Haunted High School

The Victoria Boys High School was built in 1879 on Dow Hill. During the holiday season when the school is shut down, witnesses tell stories of hearing boys running and laughing in the empty building. Some say they have seen a boy looking at them from a window. Others say they have seen a headless boy on the school grounds around the building. Nobody knows who the boy could be, as there have never been any deaths of any kind on the grounds.

Before it became known for ghosts, Kurseong was famed for its beautiful flowers. The town's name means "place of the white orchids."

Religious places, tea gardens, and museums also draw people to Kurseong.

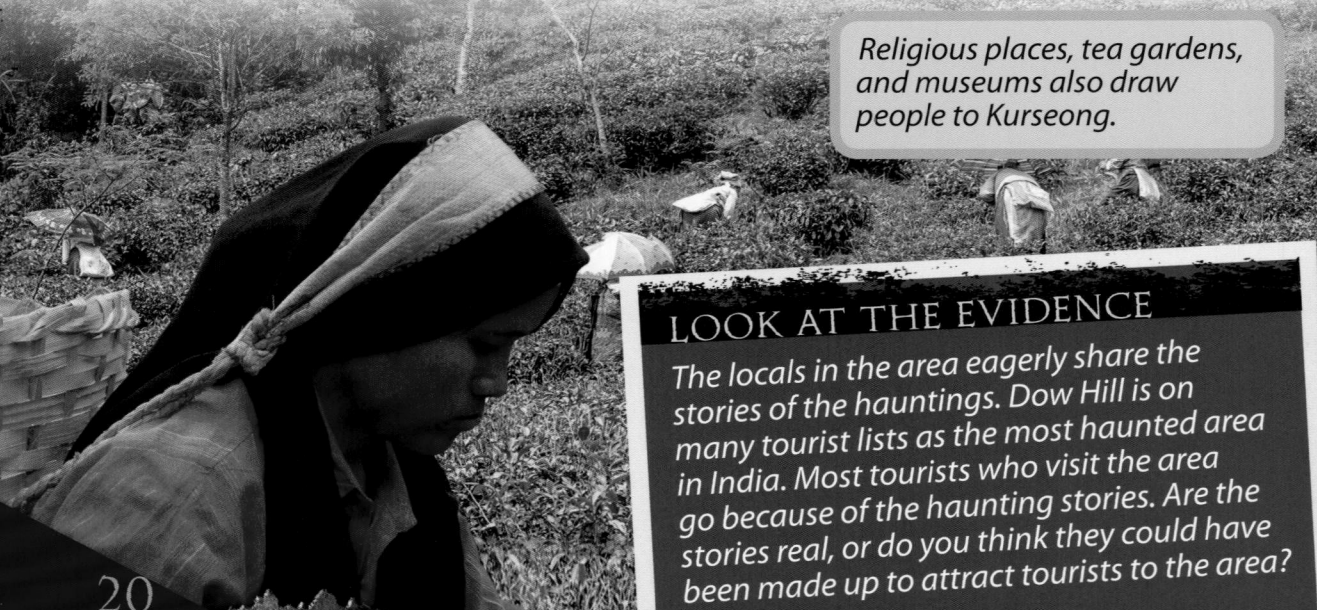

LOOK AT THE EVIDENCE

The locals in the area eagerly share the stories of the hauntings. Dow Hill is on many tourist lists as the most haunted area in India. Most tourists who visit the area go because of the haunting stories. Are the stories real, or do you think they could have been made up to attract tourists to the area?

Eerie Woods

Dow Hill itself and the surrounding forest are also said to be haunted. Locals claim to have seen a headless zombie while walking alone on the roads in the area. They say they feel like they are being followed or someone is watching them from the eerie woods. Others report hearing voices, seeing a woman in white, and seeing red eyes staring out of the dark.

One road in the area is known as Death Road. Locals report seeing a young headless boy walking on the road and disappearing into the trees. Others say they have seen the ghost of a woman with grey clothes in the forest.

According to legend, the boy zombie haunts those who see it forever and can drive a person into madness.

JAPAN'S SUICIDE FOREST

Aokigahara Forest is said to be the most popular site for suicide in Japan. As a result, it's known as the Suicide Forest. Reports estimate that up to 100 people a year die by suicide there. Some say the forest itself is responsible for the suicides. They say a "dark energy" makes visitors feel very strong feelings of sadness. The trees are twisted and close together, the ground is uneven and rocky, and there is little wildlife. The stillness of the forest adds to the strange feelings people experience there. It is said that the souls of those who die in the forest remain to haunt and torment others.

Folklore says that families in ancient Japan left sick or elderly relatives in Aokigahara during famines, or times when food was scarce, so the rest could survive. This may have started its eerie reputation.

GHOSTS OF MAMMOTH CAVE

Hidden among the forests and hills of Kentucky is the largest cave in the world. Humans have been using Mammoth Cave and its 360 miles (580 km) of passageways for over 12,000 years. Early humans used it as a burial ground. Over the years, visitors have found **mummified** bodies in the spooky cave.

Underground Maze

Tourists started visiting Mammoth Cave in the 1800s after hearing stories of the hundreds of miles of passages and the strange "mummies" that had been found there. Stephen Bishop, a young slave, was the first to explore the entire network of passages in the 1830s. He discovered the underground rivers and blind fish that live in the caverns. Later explorers found that Mammoth Cave is actually made up of a series of separate caves connected by underground passages.

DID YOU KNOW?

In the late 1700s, explorers discovered large deposits of saltpeter in the cave. This mineral is one of the ingredients for gunpowder. Slaves were used to mine the saltpeter during the War of 1812. When it ended, the value of saltpeter dropped and the mines were closed.

Mammoth Cave tours are very popular. Some visitors hope to see ghosts!

Creepy Place

Ghost stories about Mammoth Cave have been told for hundreds of years. Visitors and explorers tell of unexplained sounds, strange lights and noises, and ghosts. Why is the cave so haunted? Perhaps because of accidents that occurred during saltpeter mining. Or maybe the spirits of Native peoples and travelers who got lost in the network of caves and passages are the source of the mysterious things that happen in the area.

Mammoth Cave National Park was officially created in 1941. Although the cave continues to change due to natural events, like underground rivers wearing down rock, the stories of the ghosts and spirits of Mammoth Cave remain constant.

STEPHEN BISHOP

In 1839, Stephen Bishop, along with two other slaves, became the main explorers and guides for tourists at Mammoth Cave for the next 40 years. After that, their children continued as guides for over 100 years. Bishop is said to have refused his freedom because it would mean having to leave Mammoth Cave, which he loved.

Stephen Bishop called Mammoth Cave "A grand, gloomy, and peculiar place."

Ancient Woodland peoples gathered minerals from the caves. They made torches from cane plants to light the way. They left the caves about 2,000 years ago. Why they left remains a mystery.

Ghostly Wanderings

Rangers report seeing people dressed in old-fashioned clothing in the caverns, including the ghost of Stephen Bishop. He is buried in a nearby cemetery, and visitors say they see his ghost at night. Other say they see the ghost of Melissa. She had a crush on her tutor, but he liked another girl. She tricked him into the cave and left him. He never got out. Melissa is said to wander the cave looking for him.

Shadowy Cough

A doctor conducted an experiment in the 1840s to see if the moist air of the cave would help cure patients with consumption, now known as **tuberculosis**. He built a series of huts inside the cave. However, the trial failed when patients got worse and started dying. Visitors say that if you stand quietly near the "consumptive colony" where the patients stayed, you can hear coughing.

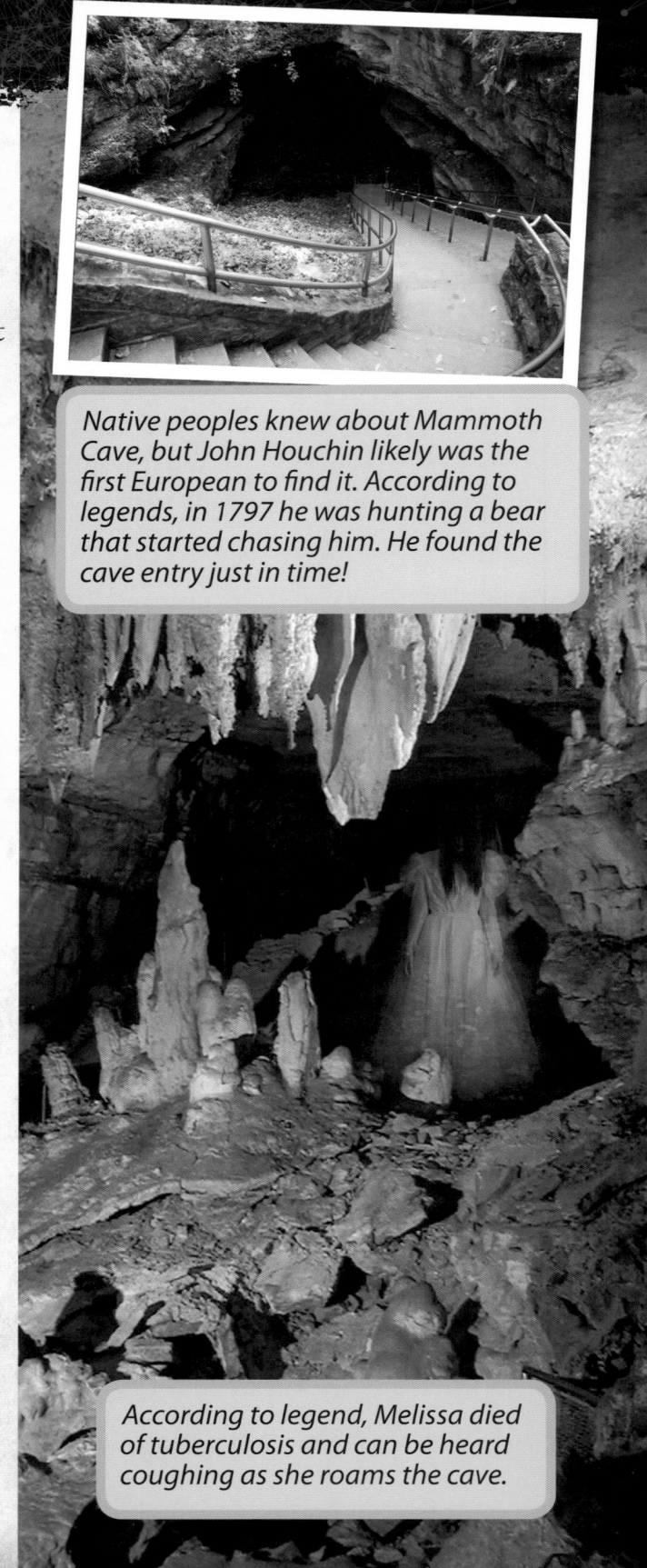

Native peoples knew about Mammoth Cave, but John Houchin likely was the first European to find it. According to legends, in 1797 he was hunting a bear that started chasing him. He found the cave entry just in time!

According to legend, Melissa died of tuberculosis and can be heard coughing as she roams the cave.

Floyd's Voice

Perhaps the scariest tale about Mammoth Cave comes from real life. Floyd Collins was a local farmer who made whiskey, which was not legal at the time. Floyd loved to explore the cave. He got trapped in 1925 when rocks fell on his leg. Rescuers tried for nearly two weeks to free him, but he died. The whole world followed Floyd's story—and continued to follow it after his death. Floyd's family and the cave's owner fought over his body. For many years, the cave's owner displayed Floyd's body to attract tourists. Then it was stolen and later found with the injured leg missing.

Finally, his family was able to bury him in a local churchyard. Even so, locals say Floyd had grown restless. Visitors report hearing his voice calling for help and begging to be rescued. Others say an old whiskey bottle was thrown at them in the area where the body was recovered.

LOOK AT THE EVIDENCE

Both Mammoth Cave and the Hellfire Caves are very popular tourist attractions that bring many people to the region. Although visitors report paranormal activity in the caves, there is little real evidence. What do you think could explain the ghost sightings and strange noises that visitors talk about?

HELLFIRE CAVES, ENGLAND

The Hellfire Caves are a network of human-made caves excavated by Francis Dashwood in the mid-1700s. Local farmers worked in the caves as miners. Dashwood was also the cofounder of the Hellfire Club. This secret society met in the caves to practice **black magic**. The Hellfire Club broke up by 1766, and the caves fell into disrepair.

During the 1940s and 1950s, the caves were renovated and turned into a tourist attraction. Visitors report hearing strange echoes and seeing ghosts appear and disappear in front of them. Others say they feel a mysterious presence in the caves. The television shows *Ghost Adventures* and *Ghost Hunters* have even conducted paranormal investigations in the Hellfire Caves.

The entrance to the Hellfire Caves was built to look like a church.

CAVE OF THE FAMOUS BELL WITCH

The Bell Witch is a famous supernatural story from American history. Legend says that John Bell and his family were living in Tennessee in the 1800s when they were attacked by a spirit of some kind. The spirit, later called a witch, could speak and change shape, and seemed to be in more than one place at a time.

Scary Kate

Bell first reported seeing a dog with the head of a rabbit, which disappeared when he shot at it. Then things started happening inside the family's home. The witch, whom they named Kate, pulled hair, slapped, pinched, and stuck pins in family members. When the family asked a neighbor to help them, the neighbor began to experience the same events. Kate soon began speaking out loud and having full conversations. People came from miles around to hear and witness the Bell Witch.

The witch continued to torment the family for several years. She threatened to kill John Bell. It was even said that she poisoned him. The witch finally left the family home, but returned seven years later.

Some say the witch was the spirit of Kate Batts, a neighbor who believed John Bell cheated her when he purchased land from her.

No Souvenirs or Else!

The old Bell farm has been rebuilt and preserved as a tourist attraction. Visitors can tour the historic Bell Witch Cave and take a haunted candlelight tour of the area.

Visitors report that they have difficulty getting their cameras to work when trying to take photos of the cave's entrance. Others say they hear whispered names and ghostly voices ordering them to leave. Legend says that anyone who takes a rock from the cave as a souvenir will have a string of bad luck.

CAVE OF SIBYL, ITALY

Cultures around the world believe that natural formations can act as a gateway into the **underworld**. The ancient Greek settlement of Cumae, near Naples, Italy, is known as the Cave of Sibyl. Legend says that a 700-year-old priestess guards the gateway and helps travelers go down to the underworld. There are deep underground vents in the rock of this mysterious and bleak wasteland. The vents release fumes and fire from nearby volcanoes. This may be why visitors over the centuries call it an "entrance to hell." Apparently, even birds won't fly over it.

Over time, the entrance to the Cave of Sibyl was lost. It was found in 1932—behind a pizza oven.

WHAT DO YOU THINK?

Do you think ghosts really exist? Some occurrences seem very convincing. When many people tell stories of seeing the same types of visions or hearing the same unexplained sounds over a long period of time, you may be convinced that the experiences are real. These stories can be very powerful.

Television shows like *Ghost Hunters* have become very popular. These shows say that anyone can look for ghosts and any unexplained light or noise could be evidence of ghosts. Paranormal investigators use high-tech scientific equipment to try to prove that ghosts exist. But there is no real scientific proof that they are actually detecting ghosts.

DID YOU KNOW?

Surveys have found that nearly half the people in the United States and Canada believe in ghosts. The numbers vary from country to country, but there are still millions of believers worldwide. Even more people think there are intelligent aliens out there. Are you one of them?

Ghosts are invited to party on the Day of the Dead. Mexican people all over the world dress up to honor the dead and bring them gifts and treats. The three-day celebration starts October 31—which is also Halloween.

Ghost Lights or Bugs?

Some occurrences may really be caused by unknown, paranormal forces that scientists have not yet been able to prove. However, some are hoaxes created by people to attract attention. The number of tourists who visit "haunted" areas is one reason why people continue to tell stories and myths about hauntings.

Other occurrences have a scientific explanation. Think back to the rusalki, or marsh nymphs, that you learned about on page 5. Many cultures describe a similar phenomenon. Some call it a will-o'-the-wisp. People tell of a ghost light often seen over bogs, swamps, or marshes that looks like a flickering lamp. Some say it's a ghost, but modern science has an explanation. Many micro-organisms and insects that live in these areas are **bioluminescent**, which means they give off light. So it's not ghosts—sometimes it's glowing bugs!

FAMOUS HOAXES

THE CAPTURED JERSEY DEVIL

New Jersey folklore describes the Jersey Devil as a kangaroo-like creature with the head of a goat, wings like a bat, horns, small arms, clawed hands, and a forked tail. People say that a baby turned into the creature shortly after birth, killing its own mother. The creature then terrorized local residents. People report hearing screams and wails from the forests and swamps in the area.

In the early 1900s, Norman Jeffries, publicist for Philadelphia's Arch Street Museum, decided to use the Jersey Devil as a way to boost attendance at the museum. He began by telling stories to newspapers about having seen the Devil. The newspapers published these stories, exciting the public. Then Jeffries and an animal-trainer friend purchased a kangaroo from a circus. They glued claws and fake bat wings to the kangaroo. Jeffries announced to the public that they had captured the Devil, and visitors could see it on display at the museum. He admitted to the hoax 20 years later.

BOOKS

Haunted Caves by Natalie Lunis, Bearport Publishing, 2012.

The Haunted Forest Tour by Jeff Strand and James A. Moore, CreateSpace Independent Publishing Platform, 2017.

Haunted Forests: Hunted in the Undergrowth: Haunted Woods You Should NEVER Enter by Hector Z. Gregory, CreateSpace Independent Publishing Platform, 2017.

Haunted Woods: Something's Out There: True Stories From Inside the Creepiest Forests On Earth by Roger P. Mills, CreateSpace Independent Publishing Platform, 2017.

WEBSITES

Top Seven Most Haunted Forests and Woods
http://theparanormal.ca/haunted_forests_woods.html

11 Haunted Forests You Should Never, Ever Step Foot In
https://thoughtcatalog.com/michael-koh/2014/10/x-haunted-forests-you-should-never-ever-step-foot-in/

Nine Haunted Caves You Can Actually Explore (But You Shouldn't)
www.ranker.com/list/haunted-caves/lyra-radford

GLOSSARY

anecdotal A personal account of something that might not be true or reliable

Bermuda Triangle An area in the Atlantic Ocean where ships and aircraft are said to mysteriously disappear

Bigfoot A big, hairy, ape-like creature that may live in western North America

bioluminescent Living organisms that give off light

black magic Magic associated with evil spirits

evidence Facts or information that indicate if something is true or not

extraterrestrial A being from a planet other than Earth

folklore Traditional beliefs, customs, and stories passed down through the generations

highwayman A thief who robs travelers on a road

hybrid Something made by combining two different elements

marsh A low-lying area often flooded and usually covered in grasses

mummified Preserved by being embalmed and wrapped in cloth

mutilate To mangle or damage violently

myth A traditional story, usually about supernatural beings or events

nymph A spirit that looks like a beautiful woman

paranormal Beyond normal scientific understanding

psychic A person who can feel things beyond the normal senses

quarry A large and deep pit where rock is or was mined

supernatural Something beyond what is accepted as normal physical laws

tuberculosis An infectious disease of the lungs

underworld The place of departed souls

werewolf A person who changes for a period of time into a wolf, often during a full moon

INDEX